Calm

a JOURNAL to self control

ELISTRIA WARREN

iCANE

Copyright © 2023 Elistria Warren for iCANE

All rights reserved. No part of this book may be reproduced
or used in any manner without the prior written permission of the copyright owner,
except for the use of brief quotations in a book review.

To request permissions, contact the publisher at iCANEmovement@gmail.com.

Softcover: 979-8-218-24728-7

First paperback edition July 2023.

Edited by Jaqueline Warren
Cover art by Elistria Warren
Layout by Elistria Warren

Scripture quotations marked NASB are from the New American Standard Bible. Reprinted by permission. Copyright © 1960, 1971, 1977, 1995, 2020 by The Lockman Foundation. (Lockman.org) Used by permission. All rights reserved.

Scripture quotations marked AMP are from the Amplified Bible. Reprinted by permission. Copyright © 1954, 1958, 1962, 1964, 1965, 1987 by the Lockman Used by permission. All rights reserved. (www.Lockman.org)

Scripture quotations marked BSB are from the Berean Standard Bible. Reprinted by permission. Copyright © 2016, 2020 by Bible Hub. Used by permission. All rights reserved worldwide. (https://bereanbible.com)

Scripture quotations marked NIV are from the New International Version Bible. Reprinted by permission. Copyright ©1973, 1978, 1984, 2011 by Biblica, Inc.™ by Zondervan. Used by permission. All rights reserved.

Scripture quotations marked NLT are from the New Living Translation Bible. Reprinted by permission. Copyright © 1996, 2004, 2007 by Tyndale House Foundation. Used by permission. All rights reserved.

Scriptures marked NKJV are taken from the New King James Version (NKJV): Scripture taken from the New King James Version. Copyright © 1982 by Thomas Nelson, Inc. Used by permission. All rights reserved.

Scripture quotations marked HCSB are from the Holman Christian Standard Bible. Reprinted by permission. Copyright © 1999,2000,2002,2003,2009 by Holman Bible Publishers. Used by permission. All rights reserved.

Scripture quotations marked WNT are from the Weymouth New Testament Bible. Reprinted by permission. Copyright © 1903. Public Domain. Used by permission. All rights reserved. (www.Biblehub.com)

Scripture quotations taken from the (LSB®) Legacy Standard Bible®, Copyright © 2021 by The Lockman Foundation. Used by permission. All rights reserved. Managed in partnership with Three Sixteen Publishing Inc. (LSBible.org) and (316publishing.com)

Learning to calm the sea of your emotions can be a very difficult task after a prolonged season of successive storms.

This journal is designed to help you process the emotions that accompany various life events and lead you to draw from the still waters of self control.

We pray you journey well.

~ Blessings

Journal Order

Introduction

Self Control : a Fruit of the Spirit

Recommendations

Notice of Intent

Foundation

Using your Journal

Survey : History

Clusters Part 1

Survey : Progress

Clusters Part 2

Closing this Chapter

Additional Pages

Introduction

Welcome to Calm

This guided journal is divided into four page clusters. Each cluster is formulated to assist you with working through life events. After each cluster, the template begins again for your convenience. We understand that life is not always simple, so additional pages are provided for you in back of the journal if needed.

Each cluster will present you the opportunity to identify and explain your feelings, name the parties involved, and express your ideal resolution. Each cluster concludes with a scripture review to provide God's perspective about your emotions. As you continue to utilize the clusters, your ease of explaining and identifying your emotions should increase.

According to your emotional state, you may choose to use the cluster as a daily tool to work through your feelings, a mechanism to revisit past life events, as a reference guide to process triggers, or an instrument to help you responsibly process conflicts.

If the event requires multiple clusters, no problem! This journal is created to be an instrument that promotes the growth of the fruit of self control in your life, assists your journey towards emotional regulation, and aids your subjection to the Spirit of God. Use as many clusters as you need to obtain your desired result.

iCANE congratulates your decision to change!

Self Control, a Fruit of the Spirit

Self control is a life saving gift from God. When David was enraged after a disrespectful encounter with an ungrateful Nabal (1 Samuel 25), he was prepared and took action to murder all the males of Nabal's household and claim what he thought was due to him. It took the quick thinking and shrewd words of a wise woman of God named Abigail (Nabal's Wife) to prevent David from taking actions that would alter the rest of his life. Her words were saturated with the sweetness of truth as she reminded him of who he was and what God promised; namely becoming King of Israel. There was no denying the truth! When his emotions settled, he thanked her for preventing his error and returned to his way [1 Samuel 30 is the evidence that David learned the value of self control].

Can you imagine what would have happened if David followed through with his plan? His reputation of valor and Godly leadership would have been tarnished, he may not have had the opportunity to take the throne as God had chosen him to do or it could have been short lived and rugged like his predecessor, he and his men would've had innocent blood on their hands with the impending consequences, a wife would have been left without a husband, and a household left without a leader.

Do you recognize how one action can trickle down to effect multiple others, even generations? The heat of the moment is no time to make life altering decisions! Take a moment to breath, come back to yourself, and remain calm.

While it is fortunate that David encountered Abigail, it is imperative that you learn to self regulate. Personal responsibility is paramount to your growth as it is unlikely that you will have a permanent companion to 'talk you down'. However, it is important to note that David succumb to the wisdom of God in Abigail because he walked in humility. The proud can only be "mastered" by God (Job 41); the highest skilled accountability will have no effect on a will that refuses to surrender to the sovereignty of God.

Mentors, Coaches, Counselors, and Pastors are invaluable resources. While we should honor their wisdom and God derived perspective, no one should be first in your life but God; this also refers to spouses. It is unwise and idolatrous to indiscriminately rely on an individual or group for direction. God is our source and He intends for us to seek His face (Psalm 105:4) and walk in His counsel (Ps 1). We are to acknowledge Him in ALL our ways and He will direct our path (Proverbs 3:5-6). Accountability should lead us back to the rock that is higher than we (Psalm 61).

Recommendations

Daily reading the Word of God helps to cultivate your character and expand your relationship with Christ. Christian Biblical sources are crucial while reading. As a general rule of mine, I suggest using a minimum of three translations while studying for complete understanding. The following are free online resources that provide definitions, context, and commentaries :

www.Biblehub.com
www.Biblestudytools.com
www.Blueletterbible.com

Though you may not be ready to trust someone with the intimacies of your deep thoughts and Spiritual journey, it is beneficial to inform a trusted person that you are on a "personal journey"; nothing else needs to be said. It is wise that one person is aware of your destination.

Finally, consider heavily your current coping skills. Coping skills are the thoughts or actions taken to manage stress. Ensure that your coping skills are healthy and promote freedom. Reciting scriptures, affirmations, and positive thoughts are excellent coping skills. They benefit many facets of your life. If a coping skill, despite its efficacy, breeds addiction or is illegal, the strong recommendation is that you cease and desist immediately. The road to freedom will not leave you bound in another area of life.

Notice of Intent

The content of this journal does not offer medical advice and is not intended to replace doctor's care. If applicable, continue to follow your care professionals instructions and/or medicinal schedule while utilizing this tool.

Foundation

To maximize the benefit of this journal, we must establish a strong foundation. There is no greater foundation than Jesus Christ and God's Word (1 Corinthians 3:11, Matthew 7:24-29). As the chief corner stone (Isaiah 28:16) and the spotless lamb (1 Peter 1:18-20), I'm more than sure that as He fulfilled the the law (Matthew 5:17 ,Romans 10:4) with with the birth, life, death, burial, resurrection, and ascension that He has given us much in the Word of God to glean from. We know that the word of God was written by men (the Apostles and Prophets), but it was inspired by the Holy Spirit (2 Timothy 3:16-17). Since the Spirit of God is the Spirit of truth (John 16:13) and Jesus and the Father are one (John 10:30), we have a sturdy foundation on which to build a structure for processing our emotions.

Foundational Scripture

1 Corinthians 6:12 (AMP) Everything is permissible for me, but not all things are beneficial. Everything is permissible for me, but I will not be enslaved by anything [and brought under its power, allowing it to control me].

Cement this truth in the forefront of your mind as you reason through your life events upon these pages.

Using Your Journal

Each four page Cluster is comprised of smaller segments that have a unique purpose: Remain Calm

The ID box at the top of the page helps you identify a specific Point of Reference for current and future processing. You may notice that as you visit an event at different ages and stages of life that your perspective changes. This is normal; as we mature and gain experience, our comprehension can elevate and shift.

Processing selection aides your recognition of repeat triggers and areas of concern. Depending on the severity of the event, parties involved, or the type of conflict, it may be necessary to process the event multiple times.

Emotional acknowledgement curtails scattered expression and holds your attention to the scale of your emotional progression during and after an event. The skill of learning to correctly identify your emotions has not been mastered by all. This will give you the practice necessary for your journey.

Naming the parties involved eases the process of admitting the circumstances to yourself and possibly identifying an abuser or instigator. Self admission is the first step to seeking further help and healing. Once you recognize the issue, you can begin to strategize against the cycle that leads to negative behaviors.

Describing the Event creates the opportunity for detailed focused recollection and the release of emotions attached to the event. It also reveals the development of the events that led your current or continued emotional status.

The <u>Re-evaluation</u> section is structured to improve your ability to recognize the benefit of reasoning through the event.

The opportunity to discern the circumstance you can and can not <u>Change</u> is critical to problem solving. Pinpointing what you CAN change will eliminate the proverbial 'spinning wheel'.

<u>Emotional Shifts</u> often happen after taking time to process. It is important for you to confirm your emotional movements for self regulation.

<u>Resolution</u> is what we all strive for but, it is unattainable at times. It is important to identify what you feel your desired resolution would be and determine if it is realistic and attainable

Every soul needs a guide to lead them to wholeness. <u>Scripture</u> remains the first and final reference guide for the Christian. Additionally, the Holy Spirit will never disagree with the word of God. Any voice, internal or external, that leads you away from scripture is not from God and not in agreement with Christ. It is integral to your healing that you know what God's word says!

<u>Surveys</u> are often used to reveal, discover, and foundation a process. The same is true in this journal. Surveys will be introduced at intervals to promote self discovery and provide a device to measure growth and progress.

Survey : History

Survey: History

How long has self control been a concern for you?

_____
_____

What is your earliest memory of "losing control"? Age _____
What happened?

_____
_____

How do you define losing control?

_____
_____

What does "losing control" look like for you?

_____
_____

What areas of your life are most effected by this issue?
(Work, Relationships, physical body, etc. List all that apply)

_____   _____
_____   _____
_____   _____
_____   _____

Are you a high conflict person?   YES   NO
Explain:

_____

_____

Who do you have the most conflict with? Circle one

   Friends   Family   Coworkers

   Strangers   Authority Figures   Subordinates

When was your last event of losing control? _____
Explain the event?

_____

_____

How did you calm yourself? Is this an old or new strategy?

_____

_____

Have you ever been successful with avoiding or resolving conflict? What strategy did you use?

_____

_____

_____

How often do you have conflicts? Circle one

    Daily   Weekly   Monthly   Quarterly

What do you feel most during a conflict? Circle One

    Fear   Anger   Rage

    Aroused   Powerful   Superior

How do you feel after a conflict?

_____

_____

_____

_____

What are your coping skills? List them below

_____   _____

_____   _____

_____   _____

_____   _____

What made you decide to address your self control issue?

_____

_____

_____

_____

Clusters : Part 1

Remain Calm

Today's Date _____
Date of Event _____
Name of Event _____
Age at Event _____

Select a phase of Processing:

☐ Beginning   ☐ Revisiting   ☐ Concluding

Emotions I felt during the Event   Emotions I currently feel

_____   _____
_____   _____
_____   _____
_____   _____
_____   _____

Who's involved?

_____
_____
_____
_____
_____

What Happened? Today's Date:_____
(Explain the event and my emotions)

_____
_____
_____
_____
_____
_____
_____
_____
_____
_____
_____
_____
_____
_____
_____
_____
_____
_____
_____
_____

Re-evaluation

Today's Date _____

Date of Event _____

Name of Event _____

What can I change about the circumstances?

_____
_____
_____
_____
_____

How do I feel after processing?

_____
_____
_____
_____
_____

What is my desired resolution?

_____
_____
_____

Do I feel resolved?   ☐ YES   ☐ NO   Explain Below:

_____
_____
_____

Scripture Review

> Galatians 5:22-23(NASB)
> But the fruit of the Spirit is love, joy, peace, patience, kindness, goodness, faithfulness, gentleness, self-control; against such things there is no law. Now those who belong to Christ Jesus have crucified the flesh with its passions and desires. If we live by the Spirit, let us also walk by the Spirit. Let us not become boastful, challenging one another, envying one another.

What is this scripture saying to me?

_____

_____

_____

Do I feel my response to the event reflects this scripture?

_____

_____

_____

How could I adjust my response to align with this scripture?

_____

_____

_____

Remain Calm

Today's Date _____

Date of Event _____

Name of Event _____

Age at Event _____

Select a phase of Processing:

☐ Beginning   ☐ Revisiting   ☐ Concluding

Emotions I felt during the Event	Emotions I currently feel
_____	_____
_____	_____
_____	_____
_____	_____
_____	_____

Who's involved?

_____

_____

_____

_____

_____

What Happened?
(Explain the event and my emotions)

Today's Date:_____

___

___

___

___

___

___

___

___

___

___

___

___

___

___

___

___

___

___

___

Re-evaluation

Today's Date _____

Date of Event _____

Name of Event _____

What can I change about the circumstances?

_____
_____
_____
_____
_____

How do I feel after processing?

_____
_____
_____
_____
_____

What is my desired resolution?

_____
_____
_____

Do I feel resolved? ☐ YES ☐ NO Explain Below:

_____
_____
_____

Scripture Review

> **Ephesians 4:26-27(AMP)**
> BE ANGRY [at sin—at immorality, at injustice, at ungodly behavior], YET DO NOT SIN; do not let your anger [cause you shame, nor allow it to] last until the sun goes down. And do not give the devil an opportunity [to lead you into sin by holding a grudge, or nurturing anger, or harboring resentment, or cultivating bitterness].

What is this scripture saying to me?

_____
_____
_____

Do I feel my response to the event reflects this scripture?

_____
_____
_____

How could I adjust my response to align with this scripture?

_____
_____
_____

Remain Calm

Today's Date _____

Date of Event _____

Name of Event _____

Age at Event _____

Select a phase of Processing:

☐ Beginning ☐ Revisiting ☐ Concluding

Emotions I felt during the Event   Emotions I currently feel

_____   _____

_____   _____

_____   _____

_____   _____

_____   _____

Who's involved?

_____

_____

_____

_____

_____

What Happened?　　　　　　　Today's Date:_____
(Explain the event and my emotions)

_____
_____
_____
_____
_____
_____
_____
_____
_____
_____
_____
_____
_____
_____
_____
_____
_____
_____
_____
_____

Re-evaluation

Today's Date _____

Date of Event _____

Name of Event _____

What can I change about the circumstances?

_____
_____
_____
_____

How do I feel after processing?

_____
_____
_____
_____

What is my desired resolution?

_____
_____
_____

Do I feel resolved?   ☐ YES   ☐ NO   Explain Below:

_____
_____
_____

Scripture Review

> Proverbs 16:32(BSB)
> He who is slow to anger is better than a warrior, and he who controls his temper is greater than one who captures a city.

What is this scripture saying to me?

_____

_____

_____

Do I feel my response to the event reflects this scripture?

_____

_____

_____

How could I adjust my response to align with this scripture?

_____

_____

_____

Remain Calm

Today's Date _____

Date of Event _____

Name of Event _____

Age at Event _____

Select a phase of Processing:

☐ Beginning　　　☐ Revisiting　　　☐ Concluding

Emotions I felt during the Event　　　Emotions I currently feel

_____　　　_____

_____　　　_____

_____　　　_____

_____　　　_____

_____　　　_____

Who's involved?

_____

_____

_____

_____

What Happened? Today's Date:_____
(Explain the event and my emotions)

Re-evaluation

Today's Date _____

Date of Event _____

Name of Event _____

What can I change about the circumstances?

_____
_____
_____
_____
_____

How do I feel after processing?

_____
_____
_____
_____
_____

What is my desired resolution?

_____
_____
_____

Do I feel resolved? ☐ YES   ☐ NO   Explain Below:

_____
_____
_____

Scripture Review

> Proverbs 15:1(AMP)
> A soft and gentle and thoughtful answer turns away wrath, But harsh and painful and careless words stir up anger.

What is this scripture saying to me?

_____

_____

_____

Do I feel my response to the event reflects this scripture?

_____

_____

_____

How could I adjust my response to align with this scripture?

_____

_____

_____

Remain Calm

Today's Date _____

Date of Event _____

Name of Event _____

Age at Event _____

Select a phase of Processing:

☐ Beginning   ☐ Revisiting   ☐ Concluding

Emotions I felt during the Event

_____

_____

_____

_____

_____

Emotions I currently feel

_____

_____

_____

_____

_____

Who's involved?

_____

_____

_____

_____

_____

What Happened?
(Explain the event and my emotions)

Today's Date:_____

_____

_____

_____

_____

_____

_____

_____

_____

_____

_____

_____

_____

_____

_____

_____

_____

_____

_____

_____

Re-evaluation

Today's Date _____

Date of Event _____

Name of Event _____

What can I change about the circumstances?

_____
_____
_____
_____
_____

How do I feel after processing?

_____
_____
_____
_____
_____

What is my desired resolution?

_____
_____
_____

Do I feel resolved?   ☐ YES   ☐ NO   Explain Below:

_____
_____
_____

Scripture Review

> Proverbs 14:29(AMP)
> He who is slow to anger has great understanding [and profits from his self-control], But he who is quick-tempered exposes and exalts his foolishness [for all to see].

What is this scripture saying to me?

_____

_____

_____

Do I feel my response to the event reflects this scripture?

_____

_____

_____

How could I adjust my response to align with this scripture?

_____

_____

_____

Remain Calm

Today's Date _____

Date of Event _____

Name of Event _____

Age at Event _____

Select a phase of Processing:

☐ Beginning   ☐ Revisiting   ☐ Concluding

Emotions I felt during the Event   Emotions I currently feel

_____   _____

_____   _____

_____   _____

_____   _____

_____   _____

Who's involved?

_____

_____

_____

_____

_____

What Happened?
(Explain the event and my emotions)

Today's Date:_____

Re-evaluation

Today's Date _____

Date of Event _____

Name of Event _____

What can I change about the circumstances?

_____
_____
_____
_____

How do I feel after processing?

_____
_____
_____
_____

What is my desired resolution?

_____
_____
_____

Do I feel resolved?   ☐ YES   ☐ NO   Explain Below:

_____
_____
_____

Scripture Review

> Philippians 4:13(NKJV)
> I can do all things through Christ who strengthens me.

What is this scripture saying to me?

_____

_____

_____

Do I feel my response to the event reflects this scripture?

_____

_____

_____

How could I adjust my response to align with this scripture?

_____

_____

_____

Remain Calm

Today's Date _____
Date of Event _____
Name of Event _____
Age at Event _____

Select a phase of Processing:

☐ Beginning ☐ Revisiting ☐ Concluding

Emotions I felt during the Event   Emotions I currently feel

_____   _____
_____   _____
_____   _____
_____   _____
_____   _____

Who's involved?

_____
_____
_____
_____
_____

What Happened?   Today's Date:_____
(Explain the event and my emotions)

_____

_____

_____

_____

_____

_____

_____

_____

_____

_____

_____

_____

_____

_____

_____

_____

_____

_____

_____

Re-evaluation

Today's Date _____
Date of Event _____
Name of Event _____

What can I change about the circumstances?

_____
_____
_____
_____
_____

How do I feel after processing?

_____
_____
_____
_____
_____

What is my desired resolution?

_____
_____
_____

Do I feel resolved? ☐ YES   ☐ NO   Explain Below:

_____
_____
_____

Scripture Review

> **Ephesians 6:10-12 (AMP)**
>
> In conclusion, be strong in the Lord [draw your strength from Him and be empowered through your union with Him] and in the power of His [boundless] might. Put on the full armor of God [for His precepts are like the splendid armor of a heavily-armed soldier], so that you may be able to [successfully] stand up against all the schemes and the strategies and the deceits of the devil. For our struggle is not against flesh and blood [contending only with physical opponents], but against the rulers, against the powers, against the world forces of this [present] darkness, against the spiritual forces of wickedness in the heavenly (supernatural) places.

What is this scripture saying to me?

_____

_____

_____

Do I feel my response to the event reflects this scripture?

_____

_____

_____

How could I adjust my response to align with this scripture?

_____

_____

_____

Remain Calm

Today's Date _____

Date of Event _____

Name of Event _____

Age at Event _____

Select a phase of Processing:

☐ Beginning   ☐ Revisiting   ☐ Concluding

Emotions I felt during the Event	Emotions I currently feel
_____	_____
_____	_____
_____	_____
_____	_____
_____	_____

Who's involved?

_____

_____

_____

_____

_____

What Happened?
(Explain the event and my emotions)

Today's Date:_____

_____
_____
_____
_____
_____
_____
_____
_____
_____
_____
_____
_____
_____
_____
_____
_____
_____
_____
_____
_____

Re-evaluation

Today's Date _____

Date of Event _____

Name of Event _____

What can I change about the circumstances?

_____
_____
_____
_____

How do I feel after processing?

_____
_____
_____
_____

What is my desired resolution?

_____
_____
_____

Do I feel resolved?   ☐ YES   ☐ NO   Explain Below:

_____
_____
_____

Scripture Review

> Colossians 3:8(AMP)
> But now rid yourselves [completely] of all these things: anger, rage, malice, slander, and obscene (abusive, filthy, vulgar) language from your mouth.

What is this scripture saying to me?

_____
_____
_____

Do I feel my response to the event reflects this scripture?

_____
_____
_____

How could I adjust my response to align with this scripture?

_____
_____
_____

Remain Calm

Today's Date _____

Date of Event _____

Name of Event _____

Age at Event _____

Select a phase of Processing:

☐ Beginning ☐ Revisiting ☐ Concluding

Emotions I felt during the Event

_____
_____
_____
_____
_____

Emotions I currently feel

_____
_____
_____
_____
_____

Who's involved?

_____
_____
_____
_____
_____

What Happened?
(Explain the event and my emotions)

Today's Date:_____

Re-evaluation

Today's Date _____

Date of Event _____

Name of Event _____

What can I change about the circumstances?

_____

_____

_____

_____

_____

How do I feel after processing?

_____

_____

_____

_____

_____

What is my desired resolution?

_____

_____

_____

Do I feel resolved?   ☐ YES   ☐ NO   Explain Below:

_____

_____

_____

Scripture Review

> James 1:19-20(NLT)
> Understand this, my dear brothers and sisters: You must all be quick to listen, slow to speak, and slow to get angry. Human anger does not produce the righteousness God desires.

What is this scripture saying to me?

_____
_____
_____

Do I feel my response to the event reflects this scripture?

_____
_____
_____

How could I adjust my response to align with this scripture?

_____
_____
_____

Remain Calm

Today's Date _____

Date of Event _____

Name of Event _____

Age at Event _____

Select a phase of Processing:

☐ Beginning   ☐ Revisiting   ☐ Concluding

Emotions I felt during the Event   Emotions I currently feel

_____   _____

_____   _____

_____   _____

_____   _____

_____   _____

Who's involved?

_____

_____

_____

_____

_____

What Happened?
(Explain the event and my emotions)

Today's Date:_____

Re-evaluation

Today's Date _____

Date of Event _____

Name of Event _____

What can I change about the circumstances?

_____
_____
_____
_____

How do I feel after processing?

_____
_____
_____
_____

What is my desired resolution?

_____
_____
_____

Do I feel resolved?   ☐ YES   ☐ NO   Explain Below:

_____
_____
_____

Scripture Review

> **Ecclesiastes 10:4(LSB)**
> If the ruler's temper rises against you, do not abandon your position, because calmness causes great offenses to be abandoned.

What is this scripture saying to me?

_____
_____
_____

Do I feel my response to the event reflects this scripture?

_____
_____
_____

How could I adjust my response to align with this scripture?

_____
_____
_____

Remain Calm

Today's Date _____
Date of Event _____
Name of Event _____
Age at Event _____

Select a phase of Processing:

☐ Beginning   ☐ Revisiting   ☐ Concluding

Emotions I felt during the Event   Emotions I currently feel

_____   _____
_____   _____
_____   _____
_____   _____
_____   _____

Who's involved?

_____
_____
_____
_____
_____

What Happened? Today's Date:_____
(Explain the event and my emotions)

_____
_____
_____
_____
_____
_____
_____
_____
_____
_____
_____
_____
_____
_____
_____
_____
_____
_____
_____

Re-evaluation

Today's Date _____

Date of Event _____

Name of Event _____

What can I change about the circumstances?

_____
_____
_____
_____
_____

How do I feel after processing?

_____
_____
_____
_____
_____

What is my desired resolution?

_____
_____
_____

Do I feel resolved? ☐ YES ☐ NO Explain Below:

_____
_____
_____

Scripture Review

> Psalms 37:8-9(NIV)
> Refrain from anger and turn from wrath;
> do not fret—it leads only to evil. For those
> who are evil will be destroyed, but those
> who hope in the LORD will inherit the land.

What is this scripture saying to me?

_____

_____

_____

Do I feel my response to the event reflects this scripture?

_____

_____

_____

How could I adjust my response to align with this scripture?

_____

_____

_____

Remain Calm

Today's Date _____

Date of Event _____

Name of Event _____

Age at Event _____

Select a phase of Processing:

☐ Beginning   ☐ Revisiting   ☐ Concluding

Emotions I felt during the Event	Emotions I currently feel
_____	_____
_____	_____
_____	_____
_____	_____
_____	_____

Who's involved?

_____

_____

_____

_____

_____

What Happened? Today's Date:_____
(Explain the event and my emotions)

_____
_____
_____
_____
_____
_____
_____
_____
_____
_____
_____
_____
_____
_____
_____
_____
_____
_____

Re-evaluation

Today's Date _____

Date of Event _____

Name of Event _____

What can I change about the circumstances?

_____
_____
_____
_____

How do I feel after processing?

_____
_____
_____
_____

What is my desired resolution?

_____
_____
_____

Do I feel resolved?   ☐ YES   ☐ NO   Explain Below:

_____
_____
_____

Scripture Review

> 1 Corinthians 10:13(NIV)
> No temptation has overtaken you except what is common to mankind. And God is faithful; he will not let you be tempted beyond what you can bear. But when you are tempted, he will also provide a way out so that you can endure it.

What is this scripture saying to me?

_____

_____

_____

Do I feel my response to the event reflects this scripture?

_____

_____

_____

How could I adjust my response to align with this scripture?

_____

_____

_____

Remain Calm

Today's Date _____
Date of Event _____
Name of Event _____
Age at Event _____

Select a phase of Processing:

☐ Beginning   ☐ Revisiting   ☐ Concluding

Emotions I felt during the Event   Emotions I currently feel

_____   _____
_____   _____
_____   _____
_____   _____
_____   _____

Who's involved?

_____
_____
_____
_____
_____

What Happened?
(Explain the event and my emotions)

Today's Date:_____

_____
_____
_____
_____
_____
_____
_____
_____
_____
_____
_____
_____
_____
_____
_____
_____
_____
_____
_____

Re-evaluation

Today's Date _____

Date of Event _____

Name of Event _____

What can I change about the circumstances?

_____
_____
_____
_____
_____

How do I feel after processing?

_____
_____
_____
_____
_____

What is my desired resolution?

_____
_____
_____

Do I feel resolved?   ☐ YES   ☐ NO   Explain Below:

_____
_____
_____

Scripture Review

> Galatians 5:13-16(NLT)
> For you have been called to live in freedom, my brothers and sisters. But don't use your freedom to satisfy your sinful nature. Instead, use your freedom to serve one another in love. But if you are always biting and devouring one another, watch out! Beware of destroying one another. So I say, let the Holy Spirit guide your lives. Then you won't be doing what your sinful nature craves.

What is this scripture saying to me?

_____
_____
_____

Do I feel my response to the event reflects this scripture?

_____
_____
_____

How could I adjust my response to align with this scripture?

_____
_____
_____

Remain Calm

Today's Date _____

Date of Event _____

Name of Event _____

Age at Event _____

Select a phase of Processing:

☐ Beginning   ☐ Revisiting   ☐ Concluding

Emotions I felt during the Event   Emotions I currently feel

_____   _____

_____   _____

_____   _____

_____   _____

_____   _____

Who's involved?

_____

_____

_____

_____

What Happened?
(Explain the event and my emotions)

Today's Date:_____

_____
_____
_____
_____
_____
_____
_____
_____
_____
_____
_____
_____
_____
_____
_____
_____
_____
_____

Re-evaluation

Today's Date _____

Date of Event _____

Name of Event _____

What can I change about the circumstances?

_____
_____
_____
_____
_____

How do I feel after processing?

_____
_____
_____
_____
_____

What is my desired resolution?

_____
_____
_____

Do I feel resolved?   ☐ YES   ☐ NO   Explain Below:

_____
_____
_____

Scripture Review

> Proverbs 15:18(NLT)
> A hot-tempered person starts fights;
> a cool-tempered person stops them.

What is this scripture saying to me?

_____

_____

_____

Do I feel my response to the event reflects this scripture?

_____

_____

_____

How could I adjust my response to align with this scripture?

_____

_____

_____

Remain Calm

Today's Date _____
Date of Event _____
Name of Event _____
Age at Event _____

Select a phase of Processing:

☐ Beginning ☐ Revisiting ☐ Concluding

Emotions I felt during the Event	Emotions I currently feel
_____	_____
_____	_____
_____	_____
_____	_____
_____	_____

Who's involved?

_____
_____
_____
_____
_____

What Happened?
(Explain the event and my emotions)

Today's Date:_____

_____
_____
_____
_____
_____
_____
_____
_____
_____
_____
_____
_____
_____
_____
_____
_____
_____
_____
_____
_____

Re-evaluation

Today's Date _____

Date of Event _____

Name of Event _____

What can I change about the circumstances?

_____

_____

_____

_____

How do I feel after processing?

_____

_____

_____

_____

What is my desired resolution?

_____

_____

_____

Do I feel resolved?　　☐ YES　　☐ NO　　Explain Below:

_____

_____

_____

Scripture Review

> **Proverbs 18:21(AMP)**
> Death and life are in the power of the tongue, And those who love it and indulge it will eat its fruit and bear the consequences of their words.

What is this scripture saying to me?

_____
_____
_____

Do I feel my response to the event reflects this scripture?

_____
_____
_____

How could I adjust my response to align with this scripture?

_____
_____
_____

Remain Calm

Today's Date _____
Date of Event _____
Name of Event _____
Age at Event _____

Select a phase of Processing:

☐ Beginning   ☐ Revisiting   ☐ Concluding

Emotions I felt during the Event	Emotions I currently feel
_____	_____
_____	_____
_____	_____
_____	_____
_____	_____

Who's involved?

_____
_____
_____
_____
_____

What Happened? Today's Date:_____
(Explain the event and my emotions)

_____

_____

_____

_____

_____

_____

_____

_____

_____

_____

_____

_____

_____

_____

_____

_____

_____

_____

Re-evaluation

Today's Date _____

Date of Event _____

Name of Event _____

What can I change about the circumstances?

_____
_____
_____
_____
_____

How do I feel after processing?

_____
_____
_____
_____
_____

What is my desired resolution?

_____
_____
_____

Do I feel resolved?　　☐ YES　　☐ NO　　Explain Below:

_____
_____
_____

Scripture Review

> 1 Peter 5:6-8(WNT)
> Humble yourselves therefore beneath the mighty hand of God, so that at the right time He may set you on high. Throw the whole of your anxiety upon Him, because He Himself cares for you.

What is this scripture saying to me?

_____

_____

_____

Do I feel my response to the event reflects this scripture?

_____

_____

_____

How could I adjust my response to align with this scripture?

_____

_____

_____

Remain Calm

Today's Date _____

Date of Event _____

Name of Event _____

Age at Event _____

Select a phase of Processing:

☐ Beginning ☐ Revisiting ☐ Concluding

Emotions I felt during the Event	Emotions I currently feel
_____	_____
_____	_____
_____	_____
_____	_____
_____	_____

Who's involved?

_____

_____

_____

_____

What Happened? Today's Date:_____
(Explain the event and my emotions)

_____
_____
_____
_____
_____
_____
_____
_____
_____
_____
_____
_____
_____
_____
_____
_____
_____
_____
_____
_____

Re-evaluation

Today's Date _____

Date of Event _____

Name of Event _____

What can I change about the circumstances?

_____

_____

_____

_____

How do I feel after processing?

_____

_____

_____

_____

What is my desired resolution?

_____

_____

_____

Do I feel resolved?   ☐ YES   ☐ NO   Explain Below:

_____

_____

_____

Scripture Review

> James 4:1(AMP)
> What leads to [the unending] quarrels and conflicts among you? Do they not come from your [hedonistic] desires that wage war in your [bodily] members [fighting for control over you]? You are jealous and covet [what others have] and your lust goes unfulfilled; so you murder. You are envious and cannot obtain [the object of your envy]; so you fight and battle. You do not have because you do not ask [it of God].

What is this scripture saying to me?

_____
_____
_____

Do I feel my response to the event reflects this scripture?

_____
_____
_____

How could I adjust my response to align with this scripture?

_____
_____
_____

Remain Calm

Today's Date _____

Date of Event _____

Name of Event _____

Age at Event _____

Select a phase of Processing:

☐ Beginning   ☐ Revisiting   ☐ Concluding

Emotions I felt during the Event	Emotions I currently feel
_____	_____
_____	_____
_____	_____
_____	_____
_____	_____

Who's involved?

_____

_____

_____

_____

_____

What Happened?
(Explain the event and my emotions)

Today's Date:_____

Re-evaluation

Today's Date _____

Date of Event _____

Name of Event _____

What can I change about the circumstances?

_____
_____
_____
_____

How do I feel after processing?

_____
_____
_____
_____

What is my desired resolution?

_____
_____
_____

Do I feel resolved?   ☐ YES   ☐ NO   Explain Below:

_____
_____
_____

Scripture Review

> **Proverbs 29:11(AMP)**
> A [shortsighted] fool always loses his temper and displays his anger, But a wise man [uses self-control and] holds it back.

What is this scripture saying to me?

_____
_____
_____

Do I feel my response to the event reflects this scripture?

_____
_____
_____

How could I adjust my response to align with this scripture?

_____
_____
_____

Remain Calm

Today's Date _____

Date of Event _____

Name of Event _____

Age at Event _____

Select a phase of Processing:

◯ Beginning   ◯ Revisiting   ◯ Concluding

Emotions I felt during the Event   Emotions I currently feel

_____   _____

_____   _____

_____   _____

_____   _____

_____   _____

Who's involved?

_____

_____

_____

_____

What Happened?
(Explain the event and my emotions)

Today's Date:_____

Re-evaluation

Today's Date _____

Date of Event _____

Name of Event _____

What can I change about the circumstances?

_____
_____
_____
_____

How do I feel after processing?

_____
_____
_____
_____

What is my desired resolution?

_____
_____
_____

Do I feel resolved?   ☐ YES   ☐ NO   Explain Below:

_____
_____
_____

Scripture Review

> Ecclesiastes 7:9 (NASB 1995)
> Do not be eager in your heart to be angry,
> For anger resides in the bosom of fools.

What is this scripture saying to me?

_____
_____
_____

Do I feel my response to the event reflects this scripture?

_____
_____
_____

How could I adjust my response to align with this scripture?

_____
_____
_____

Remain Calm

Today's Date _____
Date of Event _____
Name of Event _____
Age at Event _____

Select a phase of Processing:

☐ Beginning   ☐ Revisiting   ☐ Concluding

Emotions I felt during the Event   Emotions I currently feel

_____   _____

_____   _____

_____   _____

_____   _____

_____   _____

Who's involved?

_____

_____

_____

_____

_____

What Happened? Today's Date:_____
(Explain the event and my emotions)

_____
_____
_____
_____
_____
_____
_____
_____
_____
_____
_____
_____
_____
_____
_____
_____
_____
_____
_____

Re-evaluation

Today's Date _____

Date of Event _____

Name of Event _____

What can I change about the circumstances?

_____
_____
_____
_____

How do I feel after processing?

_____
_____
_____
_____

What is my desired resolution?

_____
_____
_____

Do I feel resolved?   ☐ YES   ☐ NO   Explain Below:

_____
_____
_____

Scripture Review

> Proverbs 19:11(NLT)
> Sensible people control their temper; they earn respect by overlooking wrongs.

What is this scripture saying to me?

_____
_____
_____

Do I feel my response to the event reflects this scripture?

_____
_____
_____

How could I adjust my response to align with this scripture?

_____
_____
_____

Remain Calm

Today's Date _____

Date of Event _____

Name of Event _____

Age at Event _____

Select a phase of Processing:

☐ Beginning   ☐ Revisiting   ☐ Concluding

Emotions I felt during the Event | Emotions I currently feel

_____   _____
_____   _____
_____   _____
_____   _____
_____   _____

Who's involved?

_____
_____
_____
_____
_____

What Happened? Today's Date:_____
(Explain the event and my emotions)

_____
_____
_____
_____
_____
_____
_____
_____
_____
_____
_____
_____
_____
_____
_____
_____
_____
_____
_____
_____

Re-evaluation

Today's Date _____

Date of Event _____

Name of Event _____

What can I change about the circumstances?

_____
_____
_____
_____

How do I feel after processing?

_____
_____
_____
_____

What is my desired resolution?

_____
_____
_____

Do I feel resolved? ☐ YES   ☐ NO   Explain Below:

_____
_____
_____

Scripture Review

Isaiah 1:18(BSB)
"Come now, let us reason together," says the LORD.

What is this scripture saying to me?

_____
_____
_____

Do I feel my response to the event reflects this scripture?

_____
_____
_____

How could I adjust my response to align with this scripture?

_____
_____
_____

Remain Calm

Today's Date _____

Date of Event _____

Name of Event _____

Age at Event _____

Select a phase of Processing:

☐ Beginning ☐ Revisiting ☐ Concluding

Emotions I felt during the Event Emotions I currently feel

_____ _____

_____ _____

_____ _____

_____ _____

_____ _____

Who's involved?

_____

_____

_____

_____

_____

What Happened?
(Explain the event and my emotions)

Today's Date:_____

_____
_____
_____
_____
_____
_____
_____
_____
_____
_____
_____
_____
_____
_____
_____
_____
_____
_____

Re-evaluation

Today's Date _____

Date of Event _____

Name of Event _____

What can I change about the circumstances?

_____
_____
_____
_____
_____

How do I feel after processing?

_____
_____
_____
_____
_____

What is my desired resolution?

_____
_____
_____

Do I feel resolved? ☐ YES ☐ NO Explain Below:

_____
_____
_____

Scripture Review

2 Timothy 1:17(NLT)
For God has not given us a spirit of fear and timidity, but of power, love, and self-discipline.

What is this scripture saying to me?

_____
_____
_____

Do I feel my response to the event reflects this scripture?

_____
_____
_____

How could I adjust my response to align with this scripture?

_____
_____
_____

Remain Calm

Today's Date _____
Date of Event _____
Name of Event _____
Age at Event _____

Select a phase of Processing:

☐ Beginning ☐ Revisiting ☐ Concluding

Emotions I felt during the Event   Emotions I currently feel

_____   _____
_____   _____
_____   _____
_____   _____
_____   _____

Who's involved?

_____
_____
_____
_____
_____

What Happened?
(Explain the event and my emotions)

Today's Date:_____

Re-evaluation

Today's Date _____

Date of Event _____

Name of Event _____

What can I change about the circumstances?

_____
_____
_____
_____

How do I feel after processing?

_____
_____
_____
_____

What is my desired resolution?

_____
_____
_____

Do I feel resolved?   ☐ YES   ☐ NO   Explain Below:

_____
_____
_____

Scripture Review

> **1 Corinthians 10:13(NLT)**
> The temptations in your life are no different from what others experience. And God is faithful. He will not allow the temptation to be more than you can stand. When you are tempted, he will show you a way out so that you can endure.

What is this scripture saying to me?

_____

_____

_____

Do I feel my response to the event reflects this scripture?

_____

_____

_____

How could I adjust my response to align with this scripture?

_____

_____

_____

Survey : Progress

Survey: Progress

The following questions refer to experiences had since the start of the journal (i.e. experiences had after initiating Clusters part 1)

Do you feel that you've made progress? Explain

_____
_____
_____
_____
_____
_____
_____
_____

What has "losing control" looked like for you since starting the journal?

_____
_____

What areas have been most triggered towards conflict?
(Work, Relationships, Physical body, etc. List all that apply)

_____	_____
_____	_____
_____	_____
_____	_____

Have you been successful with avoiding or resolving conflict? What strategy have you used?

_____
_____
_____

How have you calmed yourself after conflict? Is this an old or new strategy?

_____
_____

What do you feel during conflict?   Circle one

| Fear | Anger | Rage |
| Aroused | Powerful | Superior |

If your feelings are not present, list them below

_____

How has this changed since the last survey?

_____
_____

How do you feel after conflict? Has this changed since the last survey? Explain

_____
_____
_____
_____

What have you discovered about your coping skills?

_____
_____
_____
_____

Have you gained any new coping skills? List them below

_____	_____
_____	_____
_____	_____
_____	_____

Have your new coping skills been effective in manifesting self control?   YES   NO

Explain

_____
_____
_____
_____

Additional comments about your progress:

_____
_____
_____
_____

Clusters : Part 2

Remain Calm

Today's Date _____
Date of Event _____
Name of Event _____
Age at Event _____

Select a phase of Processing:

☐ Beginning ☐ Revisiting ☐ Concluding

Emotions I felt during the Event   Emotions I currently feel

_____   _____
_____   _____
_____   _____
_____   _____
_____   _____

Who's involved?

_____
_____
_____
_____
_____

What Happened?
(Explain the event and my emotions)

Today's Date:_____

_____
_____
_____
_____
_____
_____
_____
_____
_____
_____
_____
_____
_____
_____
_____
_____
_____
_____
_____

Re-evaluation

Today's Date _____

Date of Event _____

Name of Event _____

What can I change about the circumstances?	How do I feel after processing?
_____	_____
_____	_____
_____	_____
_____	_____

What is my desired resolution?

_____

_____

_____

Do I feel resolved?   ☐ YES   ☐ NO   Explain Below:

_____

_____

_____

Scripture Review

> **Proverbs 25:28 (HCSB)**
> A man who does not control his temper is like a city whose wall is broken down.

What is this scripture saying to me?

_____

_____

_____

Do I feel my response to the event reflects this scripture?

_____

_____

_____

How could I adjust my response to align with this scripture?

_____

_____

_____

Remain Calm

Today's Date _____
Date of Event _____
Name of Event _____
Age at Event _____

Select a phase of Processing:

☐ Beginning   ☐ Revisiting   ☐ Concluding

Emotions I felt during the Event   Emotions I currently feel

_____   _____
_____   _____
_____   _____
_____   _____
_____   _____

Who's involved?

_____
_____
_____
_____
_____

What Happened?
(Explain the event and my emotions)

Today's Date:_____

_____
_____
_____
_____
_____
_____
_____
_____
_____
_____
_____
_____
_____
_____
_____
_____
_____
_____
_____

Re-evaluation

Today's Date _____

Date of Event _____

Name of Event _____

What can I change about the circumstances?

_____
_____
_____
_____

How do I feel after processing?

_____
_____
_____
_____

What is my desired resolution?

_____
_____
_____

Do I feel resolved? ☐ YES   ☐ NO   Explain Below:

_____
_____
_____

Scripture Review

> Psalm 46:10(AMP)
> "Be still and know (recognize, understand) that I am God. I will be exalted among the nations! I will be exalted in the earth."

What is this scripture saying to me?

_____
_____
_____

Do I feel my response to the event reflects this scripture?

_____
_____
_____

How could I adjust my response to align with this scripture?

_____
_____
_____

Remain Calm

Today's Date _____

Date of Event _____

Name of Event _____

Age at Event _____

Select a phase of Processing:

☐ Beginning   ☐ Revisiting   ☐ Concluding

Emotions I felt during the Event   Emotions I currently feel

_____   _____

_____   _____

_____   _____

_____   _____

_____   _____

Who's involved?

_____

_____

_____

_____

_____

What Happened?
(Explain the event and my emotions)

Today's Date:_____

Re-evaluation

Today's Date _____

Date of Event _____

Name of Event _____

What can I change about the circumstances?

_____
_____
_____
_____

How do I feel after processing?

_____
_____
_____
_____

What is my desired resolution?

_____
_____
_____

Do I feel resolved? ☐ YES   ☐ NO   Explain Below:

_____
_____
_____

Scripture Review

> Ephesians 4:26-27(AMP)
> BE ANGRY [at sin—at immorality, at injustice, at ungodly behavior], YET DO NOT SIN; do not let your anger [cause you shame, nor allow it to] last until the sun goes down. And do not give the devil an opportunity [to lead you into sin by holding a grudge, or nurturing anger, or harboring resentment, or cultivating bitterness].

What is this scripture saying to me?

_____
_____
_____

Do I feel my response to the event reflects this scripture?

_____
_____
_____

How could I adjust my response to align with this scripture?

_____
_____
_____

Remain Calm

Today's Date _____

Date of Event _____

Name of Event _____

Age at Event _____

Select a phase of Processing:

☐ Beginning   ☐ Revisiting   ☐ Concluding

Emotions I felt during the Event   Emotions I currently feel

_____   _____

_____   _____

_____   _____

_____   _____

_____   _____

Who's involved?

_____

_____

_____

_____

_____

What Happened?
(Explain the event and my emotions)

Today's Date:_____

_____
_____
_____
_____
_____
_____
_____
_____
_____
_____
_____
_____
_____
_____
_____
_____
_____
_____
_____
_____

Re-evaluation

Today's Date _____

Date of Event _____

Name of Event _____

What can I change about the circumstances?

_____
_____
_____
_____

How do I feel after processing?

_____
_____
_____
_____

What is my desired resolution?

_____
_____
_____

Do I feel resolved?   ☐ YES   ☐ NO   Explain Below:

_____
_____
_____

Scripture Review

> 1 Corinthians 10:13(NIV)
> No temptation has overtaken you except what is common to mankind. And God is faithful; he will not let you be tempted beyond what you can bear. But when you are tempted, he will also provide a way out so that you can endure it.

What is this scripture saying to me?

_____

_____

_____

Do I feel my response to the event reflects this scripture?

_____

_____

_____

How could I adjust my response to align with this scripture?

_____

_____

_____

Remain Calm

Today's Date _____

Date of Event _____

Name of Event _____

Age at Event _____

Select a phase of Processing:

☐ Beginning ☐ Revisiting ☐ Concluding

Emotions I felt during the Event   Emotions I currently feel

_____   _____
_____   _____
_____   _____
_____   _____
_____   _____

Who's involved?

_____
_____
_____
_____
_____

What Happened?
(Explain the event and my emotions)

Today's Date:_____

_____
_____
_____
_____
_____
_____
_____
_____
_____
_____
_____
_____
_____
_____
_____
_____
_____
_____
_____
_____

Re-evaluation

Today's Date _____

Date of Event _____

Name of Event _____

What can I change about the circumstances?

_____
_____
_____
_____

How do I feel after processing?

_____
_____
_____
_____

What is my desired resolution?

_____
_____
_____

Do I feel resolved?   ☐ YES   ☐ NO   Explain Below:

_____
_____
_____

Scripture Review

> Philippians 4:13(NKJV)
> I can do all things through Christ who strengthens me.

What is this scripture saying to me?

_____

_____

_____

Do I feel my response to the event reflects this scripture?

_____

_____

_____

How could I adjust my response to align with this scripture?

_____

_____

_____

Remain Calm

Today's Date _____

Date of Event _____

Name of Event _____

Age at Event _____

Select a phase of Processing:

☐ Beginning   ☐ Revisiting   ☐ Concluding

Emotions I felt during the Event   Emotions I currently feel

_____   _____

_____   _____

_____   _____

_____   _____

_____   _____

Who's involved?

_____

_____

_____

_____

What Happened? Today's Date:_____
(Explain the event and my emotions)

_____
_____
_____
_____
_____
_____
_____
_____
_____
_____
_____
_____
_____
_____
_____
_____
_____
_____
_____

Re-evaluation

Today's Date _____

Date of Event _____

Name of Event _____

What can I change about the circumstances?

_____
_____
_____
_____

How do I feel after processing?

_____
_____
_____
_____

What is my desired resolution?

_____
_____
_____

Do I feel resolved? ☐ YES ☐ NO Explain Below:

_____
_____
_____

Scripture Review

> **Proverbs 16:32 (BSB)**
> He who is slow to anger is better than a warrior, and he who controls his temper is greater than one who captures a city..

What is this scripture saying to me?

_____

_____

_____

Do I feel my response to the event reflects this scripture?

_____

_____

_____

How could I adjust my response to align with this scripture?

_____

_____

_____

Remain Calm

Today's Date _____
Date of Event _____
Name of Event _____
Age at Event _____

Select a phase of Processing:

☐ Beginning   ☐ Revisiting   ☐ Concluding

Emotions I felt during the Event   Emotions I currently feel

_____   _____
_____   _____
_____   _____
_____   _____
_____   _____

Who's involved?

_____
_____
_____
_____
_____

What Happened? Today's Date:_____
(Explain the event and my emotions)

_____
_____
_____
_____
_____
_____
_____
_____
_____
_____
_____
_____
_____
_____
_____
_____
_____
_____

Re-evaluation

Today's Date _____

Date of Event _____

Name of Event _____

What can I change about the circumstances?

_____
_____
_____
_____

How do I feel after processing?

_____
_____
_____
_____

What is my desired resolution?

_____
_____
_____

Do I feel resolved? ☐ YES ☐ NO Explain Below:

_____
_____
_____

Scripture Review

> James 1:19-20 (NLT)
> Understand this, my dear brothers and sisters: You must all be quick to listen, slow to speak, and slow to get angry. Human anger does not produce the righteousness God desires.

What is this scripture saying to me?

_____
_____
_____

Do I feel my response to the event reflects this scripture?

_____
_____
_____

How could I adjust my response to align with this scripture?

_____
_____
_____

Remain Calm

Today's Date _____

Date of Event _____

Name of Event _____

Age at Event _____

Select a phase of Processing:

☐ Beginning   ☐ Revisiting   ☐ Concluding

Emotions I felt during the Event   Emotions I currently feel

_____   _____

_____   _____

_____   _____

_____   _____

_____   _____

Who's involved?

_____

_____

_____

_____

_____

What Happened?
(Explain the event and my emotions)

Today's Date:_____

_____
_____
_____
_____
_____
_____
_____
_____
_____
_____
_____
_____
_____
_____
_____
_____
_____
_____

Re-evaluation

Today's Date _____

Date of Event _____

Name of Event _____

What can I change about the circumstances?

_____
_____
_____
_____

How do I feel after processing?

_____
_____
_____
_____

What is my desired resolution?

_____
_____
_____

Do I feel resolved? ☐ YES ☐ NO Explain Below:

_____
_____
_____

Scripture Review

> Galatians 5:13-16(NLT)
> For you have been called to live in freedom, my brothers and sisters. But don't use your freedom to satisfy your sinful nature. Instead, use your freedom to serve one another in love. But if you are always biting and devouring one another, watch out! Beware of destroying one another. So I say, let the Holy Spirit guide your lives. Then you won't be doing what your sinful nature craves.

What is this scripture saying to me?

_____
_____
_____

Do I feel my response to the event reflects this scripture?

_____
_____
_____

How could I adjust my response to align with this scripture?

_____
_____
_____

Remain Calm

Today's Date _____

Date of Event _____

Name of Event _____

Age at Event _____

Select a phase of Processing:

☐ Beginning   ☐ Revisiting   ☐ Concluding

Emotions I felt during the Event   Emotions I currently feel

_____   _____
_____   _____
_____   _____
_____   _____
_____   _____

Who's involved?

_____
_____
_____
_____
_____

What Happened? Today's Date:_____
(Explain the event and my emotions)

_____
_____
_____
_____
_____
_____
_____
_____
_____
_____
_____
_____
_____
_____
_____
_____
_____
_____

Re-evaluation

Today's Date _____

Date of Event _____

Name of Event _____

What can I change about the circumstances?

_____
_____
_____
_____
_____

How do I feel after processing?

_____
_____
_____
_____
_____

What is my desired resolution?

_____
_____
_____

Do I feel resolved?   ☐ YES   ☐ NO   Explain Below:

_____
_____
_____

Scripture Review

> **Ecclesiastes 10:4(LSB)**
> If the ruler's temper rises against you, do not abandon your position, because calmness causes great offenses to be abandoned.

What is this scripture saying to me?

_____
_____
_____

Do I feel my response to the event reflects this scripture?

_____
_____
_____

How could I adjust my response to align with this scripture?

_____
_____
_____

Remain Calm

Today's Date _____

Date of Event _____

Name of Event _____

Age at Event _____

Select a phase of Processing:

☐ Beginning   ☐ Revisiting   ☐ Concluding

Emotions I felt during the Event   Emotions I currently feel

_____   _____

_____   _____

_____   _____

_____   _____

_____   _____

Who's involved?

_____

_____

_____

_____

_____

What Happened?
(Explain the event and my emotions)

Today's Date:_____

_____

_____

_____

_____

_____

_____

_____

_____

_____

_____

_____

_____

_____

_____

_____

_____

_____

_____

_____

Re-evaluation

Today's Date _____

Date of Event _____

Name of Event _____

What can I change about the circumstances?

_____

_____

_____

_____

How do I feel after processing?

_____

_____

_____

_____

What is my desired resolution?

_____

_____

_____

Do I feel resolved?   ☐ YES   ☐ NO   Explain Below:

_____

_____

_____

Scripture Review

> Proverbs 15:1(AMP)
> A soft and gentle and thoughtful answer turns away wrath, But harsh and painful and careless words stir up anger.

What is this scripture saying to me?

_____

_____

_____

Do I feel my response to the event reflects this scripture?

_____

_____

_____

How could I adjust my response to align with this scripture?

_____

_____

_____

Remain Calm

Today's Date _____
Date of Event _____
Name of Event _____
Age at Event _____

Select a phase of Processing:

☐ Beginning ☐ Revisiting ☐ Concluding

Emotions I felt during the Event   **Emotions I currently feel**

_____   _____

_____   _____

_____   _____

_____   _____

_____   _____

Who's involved?

_____

_____

_____

_____

_____

What Happened?
(Explain the event and my emotions)

Today's Date:_____

_____
_____
_____
_____
_____
_____
_____
_____
_____
_____
_____
_____
_____
_____
_____
_____
_____
_____

Re-evaluation

Today's Date _____

Date of Event _____

Name of Event _____

What can I change about the circumstances?

_____
_____
_____
_____

How do I feel after processing?

_____
_____
_____
_____

What is my desired resolution?

_____
_____
_____

Do I feel resolved?   ☐ YES   ☐ NO   Explain Below:

_____
_____
_____

Scripture Review

> Colossians 3:8(AMP)
> But now rid yourselves [completely] of all these things: anger, rage, malice, slander, and obscene (abusive, filthy, vulgar) language from your mouth.

What is this scripture saying to me?

_____
_____
_____

Do I feel my response to the event reflects this scripture?

_____
_____
_____

How could I adjust my response to align with this scripture?

_____
_____
_____

Remain Calm

Today's Date _____

Date of Event _____

Name of Event _____

Age at Event _____

Select a phase of Processing:

☐ Beginning   ☐ Revisiting   ☐ Concluding

Emotions I felt during the Event   Emotions I currently feel

_____   _____

_____   _____

_____   _____

_____   _____

_____   _____

Who's involved?

_____

_____

_____

_____

_____

What Happened?
(Explain the event and my emotions)

Today's Date:_____

_____
_____
_____
_____
_____
_____
_____
_____
_____
_____
_____
_____
_____
_____
_____
_____
_____
_____
_____
_____

Re-evaluation

Today's Date _____

Date of Event _____

Name of Event _____

What can I change about the circumstances?

_____
_____
_____
_____

How do I feel after processing?

_____
_____
_____
_____

What is my desired resolution?

_____
_____
_____

Do I feel resolved? ☐ YES ☐ NO   Explain Below:

_____
_____
_____

Scripture Review

> **Proverbs 18:21(AMP)**
> Death and life are in the power of the tongue,
> And those who love it and indulge it will eat its
> fruit and bear the consequences of their words.

What is this scripture saying to me?

_____
_____
_____

Do I feel my response to the event reflects this scripture?

_____
_____
_____

How could I adjust my response to align with this scripture?

_____
_____
_____

Remain Calm

Today's Date _____

Date of Event _____

Name of Event _____

Age at Event _____

Select a phase of Processing:

☐ Beginning ☐ Revisiting ☐ Concluding

Emotions I felt during the Event   Emotions I currently feel

_____   _____

_____   _____

_____   _____

_____   _____

_____   _____

Who's involved?

_____

_____

_____

_____

_____

What Happened?
(Explain the event and my emotions)

Today's Date:_____

_____

_____

_____

_____

_____

_____

_____

_____

_____

_____

_____

_____

_____

_____

_____

_____

_____

_____

Re-evaluation

Today's Date _____

Date of Event _____

Name of Event _____

What can I change about the circumstances?

_____
_____
_____
_____

How do I feel after processing?

_____
_____
_____
_____

What is my desired resolution?

_____
_____
_____

Do I feel resolved?   ☐ YES   ☐ NO   Explain Below:

_____
_____
_____

Scripture Review

> Proverbs 18:21(AMP)
> Death and life are in the power of the tongue,
> And those who love it and indulge it will eat its
> fruit and bear the consequences of their words.

What is this scripture saying to me?

_____
_____
_____

Do I feel my response to the event reflects this scripture?

_____
_____
_____

How could I adjust my response to align with this scripture?

_____
_____
_____

Remain Calm

Today's Date _____

Date of Event _____

Name of Event _____

Age at Event _____

Select a phase of Processing:

☐ Beginning   ☐ Revisiting   ☐ Concluding

Emotions I felt during the Event   Emotions I currently feel

_____   _____

_____   _____

_____   _____

_____   _____

_____   _____

Who's involved?

_____

_____

_____

_____

_____

What Happened?
(Explain the event and my emotions)

Today's Date:_____

_____
_____
_____
_____
_____
_____
_____
_____
_____
_____
_____
_____
_____
_____
_____
_____
_____
_____
_____
_____

Re-evaluation

Today's Date _____

Date of Event _____

Name of Event _____

What can I change about the circumstances?

_____
_____
_____
_____
_____

How do I feel after processing?

_____
_____
_____
_____
_____

What is my desired resolution?

_____
_____
_____

Do I feel resolved? ☐ YES ☐ NO Explain Below:

_____
_____
_____

Scripture Review

> 1 Peter 5:6-8 (WNT)
> Humble yourselves therefore beneath the mighty hand of God, so that at the right time He may set you on high. Throw the whole of your anxiety upon Him, because He Himself cares for you.

What is this scripture saying to me?

_____
_____
_____

Do I feel my response to the event reflects this scripture?

_____
_____
_____

How could I adjust my response to align with this scripture?

_____
_____
_____

Remain Calm

Today's Date _____
Date of Event _____
Name of Event _____
Age at Event _____

Select a phase of Processing:

☐ Beginning   ☐ Revisiting   ☐ Concluding

Emotions I felt during the Event   Emotions I currently feel

_____   _____
_____   _____
_____   _____
_____   _____
_____   _____

Who's involved?

_____
_____
_____
_____
_____

What Happened?
(Explain the event and my emotions)

Today's Date:_____

_____
_____
_____
_____
_____
_____
_____
_____
_____
_____
_____
_____
_____
_____
_____
_____
_____
_____
_____
_____

Re-evaluation

Today's Date _____

Date of Event _____

Name of Event _____

What can I change about the circumstances?

_____
_____
_____
_____

How do I feel after processing?

_____
_____
_____
_____

What is my desired resolution?

_____
_____
_____

Do I feel resolved? ☐ YES   ☐ NO   Explain Below:

_____
_____
_____

Scripture Review

> **Ephesians 6:10-12(AMP)**
> In conclusion, be strong in the Lord [draw your strength from Him and be empowered through your union with Him] and in the power of His [boundless] might. Put on the full armor of God [for His precepts are like the splendid armor of a heavily-armed soldier], so that you may be able to [successfully] stand up against all the schemes and the strategies and the deceits of the devil. For our struggle is not against flesh and blood [contending only with physical opponents], but against the rulers, against the powers, against the world forces of this [present] darkness, against the spiritual forces of wickedness in the heavenly (supernatural) places.

What is this scripture saying to me?

_____

_____

_____

Do I feel my response to the event reflects this scripture?

_____

_____

_____

How could I adjust my response to align with this scripture?

_____

_____

_____

Remain Calm

Today's Date _____
Date of Event _____
Name of Event _____
Age at Event _____

Select a phase of Processing:

☐ Beginning   ☐ Revisiting   ☐ Concluding

Emotions I felt during the Event	Emotions I currently feel
_____	_____
_____	_____
_____	_____
_____	_____
_____	_____

Who's involved?

_____
_____
_____
_____
_____

What Happened? Today's Date:_____
(Explain the event and my emotions)

_____
_____
_____
_____
_____
_____
_____
_____
_____
_____
_____
_____
_____
_____
_____
_____
_____
_____
_____

Re-evaluation

Today's Date _____

Date of Event _____

Name of Event _____

What can I change about the circumstances?

_____
_____
_____
_____

How do I feel after processing?

_____
_____
_____
_____

What is my desired resolution?

_____
_____
_____

Do I feel resolved?   ☐ YES   ☐ NO   Explain Below:

_____
_____
_____

Scripture Review

> Proverbs 29:11(AMP)
> A [shortsighted] fool always loses his temper and displays his anger, But a wise man [uses self-control and] holds it back.

What is this scripture saying to me?

_____

_____

_____

Do I feel my response to the event reflects this scripture?

_____

_____

_____

How could I adjust my response to align with this scripture?

_____

_____

_____

Remain Calm

Today's Date _____
Date of Event _____
Name of Event _____
Age at Event _____

Select a phase of Processing:

☐ Beginning ☐ Revisiting ☐ Concluding

Emotions I felt during the Event   Emotions I currently feel

_____   _____
_____   _____
_____   _____
_____   _____
_____   _____

Who's involved?

_____
_____
_____
_____
_____

What Happened?
(Explain the event and my emotions)

Today's Date:_____

_____
_____
_____
_____
_____
_____
_____
_____
_____
_____
_____
_____
_____
_____
_____
_____
_____
_____
_____
_____

Re-evaluation

Today's Date _____

Date of Event _____

Name of Event _____

What can I change about the circumstances?

_____
_____
_____
_____
_____

How do I feel after processing?

_____
_____
_____
_____
_____

What is my desired resolution?

_____
_____
_____

Do I feel resolved? ☐ YES ☐ NO   Explain Below:

_____
_____
_____

Scripture Review

> Proverbs 19:11(NLT)
> Sensible people control their temper;
> they earn respect by overlooking wrongs.

What is this scripture saying to me?

_____
_____
_____

Do I feel my response to the event reflects this scripture?

_____
_____
_____

How could I adjust my response to align with this scripture?

_____
_____
_____

Remain Calm

Today's Date _____

Date of Event _____

Name of Event _____

Age at Event _____

Select a phase of Processing:

☐ Beginning   ☐ Revisiting   ☐ Concluding

Emotions I felt during the Event | Emotions I currently feel

_____   _____
_____   _____
_____   _____
_____   _____
_____   _____

Who's involved?

_____
_____
_____
_____
_____

What Happened?
(Explain the event and my emotions)

Today's Date:_____

Re-evaluation

Today's Date _____

Date of Event _____

Name of Event _____

What can I change about the circumstances?

_____
_____
_____
_____

How do I feel after processing?

_____
_____
_____
_____

What is my desired resolution?

_____
_____
_____

Do I feel resolved? ☐ YES   ☐ NO   Explain Below:

_____
_____
_____

Scripture Review

> Ecclesiastes 7:9(NASB 1995)
> Do not be eager in your heart to be angry,
> For anger resides in the bosom of fools.

What is this scripture saying to me?

_____

_____

_____

Do I feel my response to the event reflects this scripture?

_____

_____

_____

How could I adjust my response to align with this scripture?

_____

_____

_____

Remain Calm

Today's Date _____

Date of Event _____

Name of Event _____

Age at Event _____

Select a phase of Processing:

☐ Beginning ☐ Revisiting ☐ Concluding

Emotions I felt during the Event   Emotions I currently feel

_____   _____

_____   _____

_____   _____

_____   _____

_____   _____

Who's involved?

_____

_____

_____

_____

_____

What Happened?
(Explain the event and my emotions)

Today's Date:_____

_____
_____
_____
_____
_____
_____
_____
_____
_____
_____
_____
_____
_____
_____
_____
_____
_____
_____
_____
_____

Re-evaluation

Today's Date _____

Date of Event _____

Name of Event _____

What can I change about the circumstances?

_____

_____

_____

_____

How do I feel after processing?

_____

_____

_____

_____

What is my desired resolution?

_____

_____

_____

Do I feel resolved? ☐ YES ☐ NO Explain Below:

_____

_____

_____

Scripture Review

> Proverbs 15:18(NLT)
> A hot-tempered person starts fights; a cool-tempered person stops them.

What is this scripture saying to me?

_____
_____
_____

Do I feel my response to the event reflects this scripture?

_____
_____
_____

How could I adjust my response to align with this scripture?

_____
_____
_____

Remain Calm

Today's Date _____

Date of Event _____

Name of Event _____

Age at Event _____

Select a phase of Processing:

☐ Beginning   ☐ Revisiting   ☐ Concluding

Emotions I felt during the Event   Emotions I currently feel

_____   _____
_____   _____
_____   _____
_____   _____
_____   _____

Who's involved?

_____
_____
_____
_____
_____

What Happened?
(Explain the event and my emotions)

Today's Date:_____

_____
_____
_____
_____
_____
_____
_____
_____
_____
_____
_____
_____
_____
_____
_____
_____
_____
_____
_____
_____

Re-evaluation

Today's Date _____

Date of Event _____

Name of Event _____

What can I change about the circumstances?

_____
_____
_____
_____

How do I feel after processing?

_____
_____
_____
_____

What is my desired resolution?

_____
_____
_____

Do I feel resolved?   ☐ YES   ☐ NO   Explain Below:

_____
_____
_____

Scripture Review

> Proverbs 14:29(AMP)
> He who is slow to anger has great understanding [and profits from his self-control], But he who is quick-tempered exposes and exalts his foolishness [for all to see].

What is this scripture saying to me?

_____
_____
_____

Do I feel my response to the event reflects this scripture?

_____
_____
_____

How could I adjust my response to align with this scripture?

_____
_____
_____

Remain Calm

Today's Date _____

Date of Event _____

Name of Event _____

Age at Event _____

Select a phase of Processing:

☐ Beginning   ☐ Revisiting   ☐ Concluding

Emotions I felt during the Event   Emotions I currently feel

_____   _____

_____   _____

_____   _____

_____   _____

_____   _____

Who's involved?

_____

_____

_____

_____

_____

What Happened? Today's Date:_____
(Explain the event and my emotions)

_____
_____
_____
_____
_____
_____
_____
_____
_____
_____
_____
_____
_____
_____
_____
_____
_____
_____

Re-evaluation

Today's Date _____

Date of Event _____

Name of Event _____

What can I change about the circumstances?	How do I feel after processing?
_____	_____
_____	_____
_____	_____
_____	_____

What is my desired resolution?

_____

_____

_____

Do I feel resolved? ☐ YES   ☐ NO   Explain Below:

_____

_____

_____

Scripture Review

> **Psalms 37:8-9(NIV)**
> Refrain from anger and turn from wrath; do not fret—it leads only to evil. For those who are evil will be destroyed, but those who hope in the LORD will inherit the land.

What is this scripture saying to me?

_____

_____

_____

Do I feel my response to the event reflects this scripture?

_____

_____

_____

How could I adjust my response to align with this scripture?

_____

_____

_____

Remain Calm

Today's Date _____

Date of Event _____

Name of Event _____

Age at Event _____

Select a phase of Processing:

☐ Beginning   ☐ Revisiting   ☐ Concluding

Emotions I felt during the Event   Emotions I currently feel

_____   _____
_____   _____
_____   _____
_____   _____
_____   _____

Who's involved?

_____
_____
_____
_____
_____

What Happened?
(Explain the event and my emotions)

Today's Date:_____

Re-evaluation

Today's Date _____

Date of Event _____

Name of Event _____

What can I change about the circumstances?

_____
_____
_____
_____
_____

How do I feel after processing?

_____
_____
_____
_____
_____

What is my desired resolution?

_____
_____
_____

Do I feel resolved?　　☐ YES　　☐ NO　　Explain Below:

_____
_____
_____

Scripture Review

> 1 Corinthians 10:13(NLT)
> The temptations in your life are no different from what others experience. And God is faithful. He will not allow the temptation to be more than you can stand. When you are tempted, he will show you a way out so that you can endure.

What is this scripture saying to me?

_____

_____

_____

Do I feel my response to the event reflects this scripture?

_____

_____

_____

How could I adjust my response to align with this scripture?

_____

_____

_____

Remain Calm

Today's Date _____

Date of Event _____

Name of Event _____

Age at Event _____

Select a phase of Processing:

☐ Beginning   ☐ Revisiting   ☐ Concluding

Emotions I felt during the Event	Emotions I currently feel
_____	_____
_____	_____
_____	_____
_____	_____
_____	_____

Who's involved?

_____

_____

_____

_____

_____

What Happened? Today's Date:_____
(Explain the event and my emotions)

Re-evaluation

Today's Date _____

Date of Event _____

Name of Event _____

What can I change about the circumstances?

_____
_____
_____
_____
_____

How do I feel after processing?

_____
_____
_____
_____
_____

What is my desired resolution?

_____
_____
_____

Do I feel resolved?   ☐ YES   ☐ NO   Explain Below:

_____
_____
_____

Scripture Review

> 2 Timothy 1:17(NLT)
> For God has not given us a spirit of fear and timidity, but of power, love, and self-discipline.

What is this scripture saying to me?

_____
_____
_____

Do I feel my response to the event reflects this scripture?

_____
_____
_____

How could I adjust my response to align with this scripture?

_____
_____
_____

Closing this Journey

Closing Survey

What have you learned about your self during this journey?

_____
_____
_____
_____
_____

What have you committed to do in this new season of your life?

_____
_____
_____
_____
_____

How will you continue on the passage to your complete Freedom?

_____
_____
_____
_____
_____
_____

Additional Thoughts?

Additional Pages

Today's Date _____

Date of Event _____

Name of Event _____

Today's Date   _____

Date of Event _____

Name of Event _____

_____
_____
_____
_____
_____
_____
_____
_____
_____
_____
_____
_____
_____
_____
_____
_____
_____
_____

Today's Date   _____

Date of Event _____

Name of Event _____

_____
_____
_____
_____
_____
_____
_____
_____
_____
_____
_____
_____
_____
_____
_____
_____
_____
_____

Today's Date _____

Date of Event _____

Name of Event _____

_____
_____
_____
_____
_____
_____
_____
_____
_____
_____
_____
_____
_____
_____
_____
_____
_____
_____
_____
_____

As you have come to the end of this journal, our hope is that your experience was enlightening and that you will continue to allow iCANE to be a part of your journey.

We pray that you have gained knowledge, insight, and understanding of self to continue your journey towards freedom and the abundant life God has planned for you.

Remain with God...He has all the answers.

Psalm 16:11

You will show me the way of life, granting me the joy of your presence and the pleasures of living with you forever.(NLT) iCANE has several tools to assist you and bare witness to your growth on your journey to freedom. From notebooks with inspirational artwork to content based materials; we are here for your encouragement..

Follow Us

for a consistent dose of teaching, encouragement, and wisdom for the storm within

   https://www.instagram.com/icane_movement/

   https://www.facebook.com/ICANEmovement

www.ingramcontent.com/pod-product-compliance
Lightning Source LLC
Chambersburg PA
CBHW050557170426
43201CB00011B/1727